Invasive species

Invasive species

Marwa Helal

Nightboat Books
New York

ISBN 978-1-937658-93-9

Design and typesetting by HR Hegnauer
Text set in Perpetua and Din
Cover Art: "Calligrabirds," by Seif Hamid

Cataloging-in-publication data is available from the Library of Congress

Nightboat Books
New York
www.nightboat.org

I will restore to you the years the locusts have eaten.

Joel 2:25

TABLE OF CONTENTS

III. i am made to leave i am made to return

I.
Invasive species

Let no one be fooled by the fact that we may write in English, for we intend to do unheard of things with it.

Chinua Achebe

poem to be read from
    right
to left

language first my learned i
second
see see
for mistaken am i native
go i everywhere
*moon and sun to
ل letter the like
lamb like sound
fox like think but

recurring this of me reminds
chased being dream
circle a in
duck duck like
goose
no were there but
children other
of tired got i
number the counting
words english of
to takes it
in 1 capture
another

شمسية و قمرية *

poem that wrote me into beast in order to be read

samira and aziza nabila awatef and 3adaal isis and ma'at yes ma'at
of the 42 laws and ideals we used to live by you of white feather
and commandment who made us taught us of stars and named
them named us made nout and systems of irrigation nile delta
source inventors of mead and kohl for drawing of lapis and woven
cloth harp sinai berber pen and paper we were winged creatures
werent we tell me because i still dream of flight sometimes i
trumpet waiting to be sound i who have made earrings of arrow
reporting now to you of the mythical creatures i dismantled in
order to become the one writing words you are reading tarsal by
metatarsal i disjointed false to be true sometimes i am cell with
eyes made up of five strand DNA quintuple helix amoeba bond
i would claim you as my ancestors thrice but once is honor i am
trying to be worthy live to have learned so much that god made
arab to know what it is to be both black and jew to be arab is to
beast in order to be read like scripture etched calligraphy wooden
metal i ask you to marvel at poetry they tried to make us forget
in guantánamo and all unnamed time will ask us of this time come
back again and again while we were out the world has become
image we made in our own image and this is what we hunt now
ive caught my reflection between incisors i beast of no nation who
want only to be read excuse me   now   it is time   to be   fed

poem for brad who wants me to write about the pyramids[1]

he says the substance is lacking a center [sic]; a traditional plot /
says [i] miss where [im] from and [i] set flashbacks while [i] walk
around san francisco / he wants to know what makes [my] story
so much more interesting and provocative than others? / says
egypt is a wonderfully exciting place ([he is] told by others) /
[he does] not like my scenes of policemen and sunflower seeds
/ says [he has] heard the pyramids are very interesting wants
to see more of egypt in my writing / / / / / / this is where the
poets will interject / they will say: show, dont tell / but that

assumes most people
most of you thought
brad is not but brad
lets him get away
understand that what
wants to see camels

can see and i bet
brad was white but
is hot so the class
with being dull but i
brad means is he
and more of his own

ideas of egypt in my work and this is how this poem becomes
its own genius annotation: see what brad missed is that i didnt
give up my spot in med school for this / and if brad had read
/ he wouldnt have missed the generous foreshadowing / would
have seen i was saying my country has become a POLICE state /
and when i say my country / i mean both / of them / the poets
will say this poem is trash / but i dont care my mother says if
you want to know what the future of the world looks like then
look to egypt and let every poem i write be a response to the
cumulus cloud of aggression that follows me and let every word
work to reverse the effect of the slow meting out of system[at]
ic violence let every letter represent a human standing in protest

1   "Some days past I have found a curious confirmation of the fact that what is truly native can and often does dispense with local color; I found this confirmation in Gibbon's *Decline and Fall of the Roman Empire*. Gibbon observes that in the Arabian book par excellence, in the Koran, there are no camels; I believe if there were any doubt as to the authenticity of the Koran, this absence of camels would be sufficient to prove it is an Arabian work. It was written by Mohammed, and Mohammed, as an Arab, had no reason to know that camels were especially Arabian; for him they were a part of reality, he had no reason to emphasize them; on the other hand, the first thing a falsifier, a tourist, an Arab nationalist would do is have a surfeit of camels, caravans of camels, on every page; but Mohammed, as an Arab, was unconcerned: he knew he could be an Arab without camels. I think we Argentines can emulate Mohammed, can believe in the possibility of being Argentine without abounding in local color." Jorge Luis Borges, *The Argentine Writer and Tradition*

poem for palm pressed upon pane

i am in the backseat. my father driving. from mansurah to cairo.
delta to desert, heliopolis. a path he has traveled years before
i was born. the road has changed but the fields are same same.
biblical green.

                         hazy green, when i say: this is the most
beautiful tree i have ever seen. and he says, all the trees in masr
are the most beautiful. this is how i learn to see.

      we planted pines. four in a row. for privacy. for
property value. that was

           ohio. before new mexico. before, i would make masr

              my own. but after my mother tells me to stop
asking her what is wrong   whenever i see her staring
out of the living room window. this is how trauma learns to
behave. how i learn to push against the page. i always give hatem
the inside seat.

      so he can sleep. on the bus.   his warm
cheek against the cold window. when i am old enough to be
aware of leaving. it is raining hard.

              5000 miles away, there is a palm. in a
pot. its leaves pressed. skinny neck bent. a plant seeking light in
an animal kingdom.

poem for the beings who arrived

Zuihitsu for Group C

if you ask me where i come from i have to converse with broken wings. this is a line. and all love is agreement, each day of living: an agree or a disagree. and love is not what we think it is. what we have been told it is: agree or disagree. i am telling you how to read me. neruda wrote: if you ask me where i come from, i have to converse with broken things. with the beings who arrived. who had the glasses of the heart. we are the beings who arrived because we had the glasses of the heart. we are the broken beings who arrived with glass for hearts. poetry is instrument; allows us to see through thought. thank you for saying my work does not sound like it is in translation, thank you for not saying my work sounds like it is in translation we are all the proof i need as singularity approaches us they ask with intrigue: how did you construct your blackness in america? each question requires a reconstruction. and i am always re never   constructed in egypt, they ask: do they hate us? i pretend not to know who they mean by they what they mean by hate but i know because i live with they and aint they. aint they? we have to stop pretending we are not [capable of] winning and i know you know we know when i dip you dip we dip this one goes out to all the women in the world you see me everywhere i go they want to know which one i am and more of? still, you see me. the mask i wear is not leo rising but the colonizer's   falling and still, you see me. and when i say you see me, what i mean is: you feel me. we, we: the beings who arrive.

in the first world

people arrive at cubicles in a rage.
at day's end, they punch
bags hanging
from the ceiling,
fight their reflections in the mirror,
sprint on padded treadmills,
while a cop sleeps outside in a car—
its engine running.

freewrite for an audience

(or reading project iii)

an alibi, an archive:

this whole reading project has been an excellent accident. i never meant to read cortázar's hopscotch in this way, with this depth or intensity. but i had left my job and my mind had some extra space as i opened hopscotch that day in the park. yes, i left my job. one day i decided i was never coming back. my heart decided for me. after some palpitations and yet another bizarre and false conversation with my boss i decided i was done. on some gone girl shit. but back to the reading, it was bolaño i had my eye on, originally. he was the one who was supposed to help me write these cubicle poems. his way with absurdity was the cure to my maladies. he was the one who wrote for the ghosts, the one who was/is (depending on whether you believe a writer lives in her writing) is/was moody as i am. writers like us, we have no plot. but then there was cortázar telling me the same story over and over again like i had been living the same day over and over again in that cube. the grey padding of the walls absorbing all my intellectual potential all my unrealized dreams. and here i am, by lottery, with you: we ended up here. first there was the lottery of birth and then i came to this country as an immigrant by green card lottery. these motherfuckers have a green card lottery while refugee babies wash up drowned at sea. but that's my next project. consider this part of my archive. when simone said to be mindful of our archives something in me resisted the idea. an archive felt like a performance, like i was supposed to be performing the act of writing instead of living it, being it. but i get it now. some things have happened to me recently that make me want to treat the archive as an alibi. see, ive seen the future, the future needs women's archives more than anything else. when they cull us, they will see it was never a man's world at all. so peace to cortázar, peace to bolaño, ive gone so far in the future im lightyears away looking back at all of us, all of the things we wanted but couldnt have. youre stars now. im a planet. they call me mars. and there is life here.

reality show

prisoner swap
al azhar's next top fatwa
the great baklawa baking show
fear factory
meet your dystopian date
weapons deal or no weapons deal
name that war
sanction this
amazing race for clean water
so you think you can poetry?
survivor: post-deportation edition

invasive species self-questionnaire

ask or aks?
depends.
        on what?
company, mood, memory,
the speed of code-
switch.

        weed or beautiful flower?
beautiful flower...growing
everywhere, anywhere, anywhere

        what happens when the colonizer's blood runs through yours?
blood type: O-
universal donor, du bois's double-consciousness;
an inner conflict. an unceasing
awareness of the gaze/a jihad of the naafs
my iranian sociology professor would say.
funny thing
about being a universal donor is
you can give everyone blood
but only take from your own kind.

        oppressed or oppressor?
complicit.
see also: under siege.

        *sand n****r or cherry picker?*
america can't even
get the slur right.

who made this taxonomy?
unmake it.

terrorist or freedom fighter?
freedom fighter. ask a real question.

when you say: "ask a real question," is that part of this performance?
yes, this is a performance of my humanity. i am saying, "look,
look at me. how intelligent i am. look, see: how i am, how i am
avoiding death."

good. because i thought for a moment, you might be possessed.
my writing is the only thing i'll let them possess.

occupation or conflict?
occupation. i said: ask a real question.
where do you want to be buried?
(i am, i am. and everywhere.) not here.

what is native?
not here.
(i am, i am. and everywhere.)

afroarab cento

*I was born a Black woman
and now
I am become a Palestinian*
    June Jordan

they know mine. I am all of them, they are all of me;
this same head knows
where all the children went when we couldn't hold it,
it doesn't matter how long you stay if you never leave.
the trouble with living like thinking is feeling is it's not
arranging all those grains of sand
in our blood. race is not biology: it is
guess the question. dream the answer.

the middle east is missing

wha do osama bin laden and i have in common?   saddam?
qaddafi? mubarak? sharon?   peres? is kashmir? is asia?
is persia? is europe? is iran? is jordan? is kurd? a language? a
religion? cuisine? borders on bordering? wha do you and i have in
common?   red sea dead sea an empire syria iraq   say kurd
say we were occupied
a people under siege of make xenophobia believe   drink and say,
"zamzam."

say we did it to ourselves.
say: complicit. i want to walk/   return maps speak to managers
of mapmakers
i'd like to see god's atlas compare it to ours trace a new equator
a river nile still running azure
azure
upwards its own gravity joins scapegoat to scapegoat
in song: *row row row your boat gently down the stream merrily merrily*
merrily life is but a dream
          x3
say je suis zidane, je suis egyptienne.

say it to a rhythm not a plot
          a quality not a toxin
say dizzy without jury without trial ask   of us just us sing back
lyric
          dust off vulgar gaslight

say it in the colonizer's tongue.   call it the cradle of civilization
say dunyah say la illahah   ila allah say jannah inscribe your
history inside every barren closet you once occupied say quickly
here we are now entertain us / cartographers agitate us

        exact us   excise us

would you make a space for me? between zoot jute epoxy and a
hard place somewhere   between vengeance and yolk next to
the place you go to quake

ive brought my own pillow plus sleeping bag but now the letters
have become cryptic i   cant tell if it is because of shyness or
lack of interest when you look like me you can say things no one
will question or everyone will question you in june as a zygote in
uterus in excess

maybe it is a cry for help. maybe it is just a cry. say palestinian
say palestine
say syria
say syrian
say baby
say future
say mine
say yemen
say yemeni
say zay (like)
say hena (here)
say mine say ghost in context weep quietly then wail
so make a space for me in your mind.
make me a space
        graph, transcribe. jaunt, wax,   wane.
here is neruda. here is his book of questions.
here is mine. a quiz of sorts. this is the map i navigate by.

who you pulling from bricks? a baby? an arm? books? a ball? who's is
it? you ask   coaxing at gallons of quicksand absorbing and vying
for joy, for protozoa

pray static pray jaw pray zoroastrian
pray xanax pray quickly borrow what you will from
god, from vagrancy, from vacancy

before i left i wrote: where you from? where you from? where you
from? inside every   empty closet of the homes i once
occupied. dont forget
where youre from, dont squint. zoom in. stow the box, lock the
key. jump on.

we made a new map from breath from zone to zone we
moved, traveled, walked,   journeyed. there are many
who experience what we havent quote benefited from being unquote.

maybe a cry for help, maybe jus a cry. maybe a memory quivering of
a juvenile   kingdom's lie, maybe was a zealous royal
who unleashed sand and sphinx making borders die: in yellow,
blue, green, and red, orange and cream lines.

the middle east experts are missing

* drops duct tape * wipes brow *

you are thinking about the last white person you had to cut out
of your life. the one who took a picture of dylann roof to the
hairdresser "coz she wanted a look with 'creeper vibes.'" you
wonder if the hairdresser was a person of color and rage fills
you. how clearly you see that murderer while the hairdresser…
and you do what you always do when this happens in public, you
dissociate switching to the fantasy of having a particular baldwin
quote[1] printed on billions of small cards and dropping them via
drone all over this country. you are fantasizing about how you are
always fantasizing about this but the quote is always changing and
the location is always changing then you are thinking on home and
language and how in some ways they have come to mean the same
thing. the train arrives, you get a seat. at the next stop a large
white man finds the open space beside you and you resist the reflex
to make yourself small, to make room for him. he shrinks into
the allotted negative space and reveals a pack of index cards with
your mother tongue scrawled on them. you remember god is a
surrealist poet and has a funny way of revealing herself to those
who will believe. but you wonder why this campy looking man has

1 "Until the moment comes when we, the Americans, are able to ac-
   cept the fact that my ancestors are both black and white, that on
   that continent we are trying to forge a new identity, that we need
   each other, that I am not a ward of America, I am not an object of
   missionary charity, I am one of the people who built the country—
   until this moment comes there is scarcely any hope for the American
   dream. If the people are denied participation in it, by their very pres-
   ence they will wreck it." James Baldwin, "The American Dream and
   the American Negro" March 7, 1965.

such an interest in your language. a slew of predictable acronyms rush to the forefront of your mind: CIA, FBI, NSA—based on his age, you dismiss the possibility of the foreign service exam. you are tempted to ask, "why such an interest in arabic?" then you notice a golden band on his ring finger. perhaps he is learning it for the love of a woman who loves this language as much as you do. this sole warm thought is fleeting, as he is: he stands directly in front of you as he prepares to exit the train. you scrutinize him. you sense he senses it. you want to make him uncomfortable. you want to know what he is going to do with your language. but you do not ask. you go home and write this instead.

multiplication of the blues

after Philip Metres after Sand Opera

you, you: lynddie, you. lynddie: manipulatedanipulator. i made
a new word for you. ive known you from that small town. went
to high school with a girl like you. you never were too good at
math; a multiplication of the fools. never would have imagined
you, of all people, on the big tv news. but life's got a fancy
calculator and you caught a case of 'be all you can be' attitude.
counting hoods on pointed fingers… all those things he made you
do. lynddie, you damn fool. i would have helped you cheat on
math. could have told you he was cheating you. girl, they played
you like the saddest kentucky blues. now, now, lynddie lou. you
made a deal with the devil while singing: "*anything he asked/ he
knew/ i would do.*" but did you, lynddie, did you have to make a
baby with him too?

dreamwork

after Philip Metres after Sand Opera

poems do work journalism cant and dreams do work only dreams
do. in waking, i skim headlines. one reads: "guantánamo detainee
refuses offer of release after 14 years in prison." the one who wrote
it, his name is "savage." which is real? which is dream? the unlikely
is likely in reality and in dreaming. journalism is the work of the
sleeping. poetry is the work of the dreaming. we each arrive in the
same dream differently: in one the fly goes unnoticed; in another
the fly is swatted; the fly crumples; the fly goes free; the prisoner
is waking in the unacknowledged legislator's dream.

)[[:".'.,:]](REMIXED

after Philip Metres after abu ghraib arias and
set to the disintegrating instrumental ballet
of ███████ *'s "Runaway"*

some / some
where / where
on the other
side of these
words are heart chambers where they are gasping clenching
clutching for air just air as we stare all we do is stare and stars
stare back with eyes inverted as nout exits day exits night exits day
have you seen ancient temples where confusion transforms into
clarity black sights doubts knowing feeling drawing shapes from
punctuated forgetting diffusion is a healing through the slippery
osmosis count sheets of music on music of music and wash their
atomic
weight / weight
wait / wait
i remember
the pythagorean theorem is good for shortcuts so find the next mark
a reminder of how intelligent we are so intelligent it is frightening
us not knowing how we know what we know that we know what
theyre thinking and it paranoias us as verb is reaction on their
faces these familiar faces in the punctuation of all things left unsaid
there are bodies punctuated souls in the punctuation tell me what
is seeing without light country without military without america a
guantánamo building a new relationship with cuba to the tune of
gil scott heron rapping about a new route to china what is vitality
if a life is forced between brackets an ending of lyric so quote
your ability to forget and contract a concentration connecting you

thought id say camp to remind you of our humanity so put a halo
on because we are holograms the holograrabs of abu ghrairabs at
this point you should be concentrating like juice in a box and grab
a colon while youre at it a colon a colon separates thought there
is always separation c r e a t i n g distance in d i s t a n c e there
is leaving and in leaving there is seeing reflecting the function' of
punctuation connecting and separating indicating the signs youve
been looking for in what has not yet been written so save it while
you listen to the ones who need saving do you hear them they are a
symphony arriving and you are singing in this chorus of complicit
a choir not of church nor of ameen in collective prayer not of
scratchy microphones at dawn or of the silence before we break
fast it is their chorus when i can see music in a constellation and
your name is an aria so please join in this recitative and dont let go

dont / dont

let / let

go

:

:

[   ]   [

]

"

let's get this out the way

i find it impossible to compensate for these long absences in any
way. i have spent all of my life leaving, i have made art of it.
now, to study returning.
these places dont go anywhere, but we do.
passion is specific.
love is not linear.

the brightest years were the darkest years.
the darkest years were the brightest years.

i feel my absence, i feel my presence.
brevity implies intimacy.
brooklyn, new york is the place ive lived the longest in my life.
i once calculated the total percentage spent here; it came to 17.
a barely respectable dining tip in this city.
over the past seven years ive watched my face age slowly in the
reflection of the train windows.
distance is the story ive always wanted to tell.
so, ill tell it now.

II.

Immigration as a Second Language

Right now, a tiger named Andrea who lives in the Portland Zoo is dying of cancer in her uterus. The zookeepers might have caught the disease earlier if only she hadn't kept it hidden, but animals are programmed not to give away their symptoms lest their predators take notice and begin the chase. There is a biological imperative that drives us not to show any traces of our pains, not to reveal any clues about our grip on existence having weakened. In the wild, the lame are quickly eaten, an efficient solution to the problem of disease, without even a need for cleaning up, thanks to the carrion-eaters and then the microbes.

It's probably because I studied wildlife biology in college that my mind tends to drift in the direction of wondering what my life would be like if I were a wild animal.

from "A Glimpse," *I've Heard the Vultures Singing*, Lucia Perillo

I remember the second time I immigrated to this country.
I do not remember the first.

Security Screening:

Once you have gone through security
follow the signs to the appropriate
waiting room.

Aged out—that's what happened when I turned 21. While other kids were stressing about buying cases of Natty Light with fake IDs, I was processing my very own, independent, student, J-1 visa.

Or my father, stunned, when I recall him whispering a prayer, face up toward the ceiling in an immigration office in Cleveland.

"It's what the law is," the officer says. "I'm sorry."

Or should I start with anthrax? It's one of the reasons our application was destroyed in an I.N.S. office in Washington, D.C., causing a "delay" in "processing" my parents' green cards, which in turn delayed my own.

Aging out occurs when minor children lose their eligibility for immigration benefits as a result of I.N.S. processing delays.

Our application thrown out, destroyed without any notification from the immigration office in Washington, D.C.

I remember the drive—all the early morning and afternoon quiet gray.

A denial: Though my mother has received her green card through lottery (making my father, me, and my brothers eligible too) we are denied because my father has not fulfilled his J-2 Visa residency requirement—a requirement that he return to Egypt for two years before adjusting immigration status. (see: letter J)

"How do you remember that?" my father asks when I remind him of that officer years later.

A-L-I-E-N in smudged black typeface on my social security card. Seeing the word printed like that. Confirmed what I already felt.

a·sy·lum

ə'sīləm/

noun

noun: **asylum**; noun: **political asylum**; plural noun: **political asylums**; plural noun: asylums

1. the protection granted by a nation to someone who has left their native country as a political refugee.

   "she applied for asylum and was granted refugee status"

   • shelter or protection from danger.

      "we provide asylum for those too ill to care for themselves"

   synonyms: refuge, sanctuary, shelter, safety, protection, security, immunity; a safe haven

   "he appealed for political asylum"

2. *dated*

   • an institution offering shelter and support to people who are mentally ill.

      "he'd been committed to an asylum"

   synonyms: psychiatric hospital, mental hospital, mental institution, mental asylum; *informal* madhouse, loony bin, funny farm, nuthouse, bughouse;

   dated lunatic asylum;

   archaic bedlam

   "he was confined to an asylum"

Origin

late Middle English (in the sense "place of refuge," especially for criminals): via Latin from Greek *asulon* "refuge," from *asulos* "inviolable," from a- "without" + *sulon* "right of seizure." The current senses date from the 18th century.

Birthplace: Al Mansurah, Egypt. Al Mansurah lies on the East bank of the Damietta branch of the Nile in the Delta region. It is 120km northeast of Cairo.

I was 2.5 when I came to the U.S. with my family. In 1983, my father received a fellowship to complete his doctoral studies at The Ohio State University. He was 29, my mother 22. She, my three-month-old brother and I joined him. There was always the promise of going back but my father took longer than expected to complete his research, and by then my brother and I had become accustomed to America.

They decided to stay, even after they enrolled us in schools back in our Egyptian hometown. They didn't want to disrupt our lives. Throughout, they remained legal, documented.

First English word? "Geoffrey." The Toys "R" Us giraffe. I learned English watching TV. My parents realized this when I kept repeating, "Geoffrey! Geoffrey!" as I smacked my hands against the car window, as we drove by a Toys "R" Us in Columbus, Ohio.

First memory in America? My Head Start classmate, one of my first friends[1], forcing a blue thumbtack into his forehead. Then screaming loudly. Our teachers are rushing over.

---

1   Does it make a difference to mention he is Black?

Census. In the summer of 2000, there was a knock on our front door. Then the doorbell rang. My father answered it, "Hel-lo."

"Hi, I'm from the Census Bureau—do you have a few moments to answer a few follow-up questions about your Census form?"

"Shoor."

She looked down at her clipboard. "Well, Sir, it looks like you checked a few boxes for race, although it says there are only five people in your household."

"Yess?"

"How is that possible?"

Previously, my father had checked the form: White Non-Hispanic, African, African-American, Multiracial, and Other.

"Hang on, please. Just one second." He loudly called out, "yaa Aaazza, Maarrrwaa, Haaatem, Yaassserrr..." We gathered at the entrance in the order he had called us. "Look at my family and tell me what you see." A Biology professor, my father enjoyed challenging his students in the same way. She looked over our faces, each of us a different shade ranging from my mother's ivory skin to my father's dark summer brown—my brothers and me the gradients between.

My father went on with his lesson (she may as well have come over to ask about the binomial nomenclature of some plants in the yard). "We are from Egypt." A fan of the Socratic method, he went on. "Do you know where Egypt is?"

"Africa?" She replied hesitantly.

"Would this qualify us as African-American?" He didn't wait for her answer this time. "We get mistaken for just about everything around here and not one of us is the same color as the other. So," he paused. "I checked everything that applied..."

By 1924, there were about 200,000 Arabs living in the United States[2] and by 2000, at least 3.5 million Americans were of Arab descent[3].

It is 2010. A census form arrives in the mail.
I check OTHER and write-in: A-R-A-B.

2 "Arab-American History." 2010. Arab-American National Museum. N.p., Web. 29 Apr 2010.
3 "Arab-American Demographics." 2010. Arab American Institute. N.p., Web. 16 May 2010.

In 2016, Obama wants to add a new racial category and has chosen an acronym to describe a group of people: MENA (Middle Eastern and North African)[4].

I note the absence of the word "Arab."

Still, they do not sense us[5].

4 "...as it's called by population scholars — is broader in concept than Arab (an ethnicity) or Muslim (a religion). It would include anyone from a region of the world stretching from Morocco to Iran, and including Syrian and Coptic Christians, I[----]li Jews and other religious minorities." excerpt: "White House wants to add new racial category for Middle Eastern people," Korte, Gregory, USA Today. N.p., Web. 30 Sept 2016.

5 "US Census fails to add MENA category: Arabs to remain 'white' in count." 2018. N.p., Web. 27 Jan 2018.

Dream. In the summer of 2005 I had a recurring dream in which I was looking out of an elaborate skyscraper made entirely of glass.[6] I could hear two helicopters beating through the air in the distance and everything in sight was burning, burning. Smoke and flames. I looked on knowing that eventually the flames would engulf me.

Images of immigrant stereotypes flooded my mind: the migrant worker sitting on a paint bucket waiting for a ride and a day's work to begin; the fruit pickers sweeping through fields at dawn; others slaving in sweatshops; in assembly lines; packed in vans; sharing tiny apartments in New York City; cab drivers; fruit stand vendors; the hot dog stand guys; forged passports—thousands spent on fake IDs, green cards; whatever it took: sneaking on boats, trucks, crawling over, under, through fences.

Day after day, I had placed my right hand over my heart, pledging allegiance to the "United States of America, and to the republic for which it stands, one nation under God, indivisible, with liberty and justice for all." I was a National Honors Society student; captain of my Midwestern division three state qualifying tennis team; family vacations in Miami and Clearwater Beach (before MTV knew where it was); horseback riding in the Smoky Mountains; Disneyworld, Magic Mountain, pictures with Mickey and Minnie; summers spent fishing in Lake Erie and swimming in Lake Michigan; sunsets over the Golden Gate Bridge; a volunteer taking vitals at the local hospital's emergency room, holding

6   Construction on the Freedom Tower begins in 2006. I recognize it as the
     building from this dream.

babies down for stitches; your friendly college dorm room RA; leaf-raking, waving-hello-suburban-next-door neighbor.

Deportation. I had 180 days until I would be deemed an "illegal alien," a statistic—one of nearly 11 million people in the U.S.

Embassy: the main office for the American government located in a friendly foreign country.[7]

Ex. Some people have adverse reactions to doctor and dentist visits but for me, it's embassies.

In that same summer of 2005, like a stray cat headed to the vet's office, I packed for Egypt, planning to come back to the U.S. to reluctantly begin a master's degree in Near Eastern Languages and Cultures at Ohio State University. I would need a new visa to do so, so I went to the U.S. Embassy in Cairo to apply for one.

July 10, 2005 6:00 am

The sun is still rising as we drive to Cairo for my appointment at the embassy. It is 6:00 am.

My mother and I share the backseat of my father's favorite driver's cab, Mohsen Ali. My father has made these arrangements from Ludington, Michigan where he is teaching summer courses in fish and lake biology.

The tune "It's a Small World After All," blares from the small blue Nokia cell phone my mom borrowed from one of my cousins the night before, breaking the peaceful silence in the cab each time one of my anxious aunts calls to check on us. My mom ignores the phone—and predictably, Mohsen Ali's phone rings shortly thereafter.

My family always refers to him by his full name so as not to confuse him with the dozens of other Mohsens in our hometown.

---

7 "American Visa Glossary: American Visa Bureau" N.p., 29 Apr 2010. Web.

because of the number of Mohsens we know in our hometown. He is a long-bearded fellow who always wears white or gray galabiyahs, and believes all women should wear higab. My mother detests his stifling conservatism and gives my father a hard time for employing him. His presence is oppressive and adds a depressing tone to our morning quiet. My mother and I each look out our car windows, my eyes drinking in the neverending fields that grow along the Nile tributaries as we rush past. This is the place I travel to in my best dreams.

An hour and a half later the green fields and tributaries transform into a corniche separating the city from the Nile. We enter downtown Cairo at sunrise. The phone is still ringing. A smoggy haze sits above the river and I admire the feluccas docked along the water's edges. The streets are empty save a few traffic officers.

We continue to drive along the corniche into Garden City. It's a small affluent neighborhood that houses almost all of the western embassies, each of them barricaded behind high walls.

Officers in black and green uniforms scrutinize us as we navigate through the turns of the metal security fences.

It is a few minutes past 7:20 and there is already a line outside of the American Embassy, though the first appointments begin at 8:00 am. I know this because I have called the "Embassy hotline" many times leading up to this day. Two imposing guards with AK-47s stand on either side of the entrance.

At the door, an embassy official announces that only applicants with appointment papers can enter. I tell my mom I'll keep her posted via text.

They search my bag and put me through a metal detector. Finally, they ask for my cell phone. They take it and tell me I can pick it up on my way out.

I'm wearing my favorite black wash jeans and a khaki sleeveless shirt with a striped blazer—part of a suit I rarely wear—bought in Washington, D.C. for a job interview at ABC News.

I follow the brass signs to the consulate section.

As I pass through the first narrow hallway I notice two pairs of eyes on either side of me.

Two American national guardsmen stare down from their posts behind the glass.

Later, my mind slowly calculates the value of bodies: Egyptian guards outside. American inside. Underground. Behind bulletproof glass.

Then a dim winding hallway.

Down some stairs.

Consulate section: protected, underground, windowless.

The the small consular booths with their impassable glass and the large dark blue numbers over them. Two adjacent walls are dedicated to these numbered booths.

Rows of metal chairs run through the center of the space. Lines have already formed.

There is a coffee cart with snacks beside the door. I notice the man at the cart is the only person at ease in the entire place. Everyone else clutches or riffles through files. The ones with children are trying to keep them quiet.

I am instructed by a young American intern to turn my passports and application in at Window 2. I do so and then am told to wait.

As I look for a place, to sit I notice an unusual number of Copts wearing large silver and gold crosses around their necks or holding rosary beads—more than I've seen together in all my time in Egypt. This is the right place to flaunt your Christianity.

I sit next to an elderly woman who smiles at me and asks why I am going to Amreeka. I tell her, to complete my graduate studies. She figures my English is good enough and asks for help filling out one of her forms.

When a Coptic priest overhears us, he asks me to help him memorize the pronunciation of the street name he will be staying on. Between chatting with them, I suspiciously eye a young Egyptian man in a navy blue suit and a blonde woman in a flowery dress (their fake green card marriage discomfort blaring).

My thoughts are interrupted when I'm called to Window 7 for fingerprints.

And then I'm sent back to wait.

Around 2:00 p.m. I am called to Window 6.

The consular officer, a Black woman with long braids asks me several questions in an efficient manner. I do my best to respond in the same manner. She then hands me a ticket to claim my student visa, but then she backtracks after spotting something in the computer and asks me to return the ticket she had just handed me. I can barely hear her say something about how I'm not, "answering her questions directly" to another officer. She then returns to me and I am told to sit and wait.

I sit and wait.

The hall slowly empties.

One by one, the people I have spoken to throughout the day are leaving. Even the guy with the snack cart. It is just me.

I miss the people breathing down each other's necks. I am scared and worried. I hear my stomach rumbling. It is the only thing I can hear. I hadn't thought to eat. I thought this would be quick.

Around 5:00 p.m., a white man says loudly enough for me to hear through the bulletproof glass say, "What the hell is she doing here?"

He doesn't know I can hear him. Rather, he probably doesn't realize I can understand him.

The woman with braids rises from her desk, hands him some paperwork and says something inaudible.

A few minutes later an officer hands me a yellow ticket requesting that I come to the consular section and to bring both my parents the next morning at 8:00 a.m.

She is Egyptian and I trustingly explain that I need to make another appointment because an 8:00 a.m. appointment is impossible. We are from Mansurah, I explain and need more time to allow for the distance, the travelling.

She accommodates my request and reschedules it for 10:00 a.m. the following morning.

On my way out, I find the booth to retrieve my cell phone.

A fat, balding man hands it back to me and asks me where I'm from.

I have been cut off from communicating with anyone for the past nine hours and he wants to know where I'm from.

I glare at him.

I deny myself the much needed moment of comic relief, as I realize: no matter where I am, the question never changes. The question is an uncomfortable home of sorts.

I turn the phone on to call my mom and find all the credit I had has been depleted.

Exiting the cement embassy, my mother is the only one there. She is crouched on a stoop under the awning of a closed souvenir shop. Her face is sunburnt, her eyes tired. She is tired. She looks at me expectantly for news. I tell her they've asked me to come back tomorrow and to bring her with me.

Visit Two: July 11, 2005 10:00 a.m.

My mother and I go to the embassy. My mom wears an insulin pump and there is a lot of ruckus about it at security.

Around 11:30 we are called to Window 2 where we present our packet of IAP-66 forms/DS-2019s, paperwork that proves our stay in the U.S. was legal.

I'm told my application won't be denied, but to bring my father during my next appointment, should I choose to schedule another one.

The consular officer during this trip is cordial, understanding.

Though I don't understand why they keep asking for my parents when I am now over 21 years of age.

Visit Three: July 21, 2005 10:00 a.m.

I arrive with both my parents. My father flew in from the U.S. specifically for this. It's clear the officer has made up her mind before she sees my file.

"Did you burn your old passports?" she asks my father.

"Do you have health insurance?" she angrily asks my mother.

I'm not sure what this has to do with my application. I can't remember what she's asked me, what I'm trying to answer when she says, "I'll refuse you for the fun of it."

My application is turned away (not denied—it's as if they never saw it, as if I had never been there at all—erased, gone). Like the anthrax but this time I'm here for it.

Witnessing my own erasure.

I am standing in front of her with my parents and every passport of mine, every convoluted acronym-ed form I've had to my name when she hands me the following memo:

> "The Consular Section regrets that it is unable to issue a non-immigrant visa to you because you have been found ineligible under section 214(b) of the Immigration and Nationality Act. Section 214(b) of the Act requires applicants for non-immigrant visas to show a permanent residence abroad and intent to depart the United States at the end of the authorized stay. Unfortunately, you have not shown that you have sufficient family, social, or economic ties to your place of residence to ensure that your projected stay in the United States will be temporary.
>
> No further consideration can be given to your visa application unless at a later date you have new information to present. You were not refused because you were asked for documents and were unable to present them during your interview with the consular officer."

Knowing this isn't how it is supposed to end, I stay standing on my side of the window, "What's your name?" I ask.

She turns to leave while *shooing* me away with a wave of her hand, a snotty, "Buh-bye."

"Can I have your business card?" I ask.

"It's time to go," she says and walks away.

Over a decade later, I tell my therapist how I understand intimately why those windows are bulletproof. I am not emotional when I say this. I say it with a coolness. As if I have shot through them hundreds of times.

Wednesday, August 17, 2005 at 9:09:57 AM

Ms. Mancilla and Ms. Plaster:

Hope you're well. Thank you for taking the time to intervene on my behalf with the American consulate in Cairo, Egypt. I have just received the response from the embassy on Friday, August 12, 2005. The embassy has only restated the same reasons for the denial which we have come to understand, but will not accept.

I presented the embassy with as much evidence as any 24-year-old woman in Egypt has to her country. My only mistake being that I have been in the United States since I was a child, due to my family's circumstances.

My family and I came to visit your office in March of this year because of our rare circumstances and as an attempt to avoid the problem we are encountering now. I applied for a fresh, independent student visa and am being penalized for a decision I could not have made for myself (as a child). I am requesting that your office continue to intervene, by convincing the consulate to look at my circumstances as an independent adult, and minimizing the effects of my parents' decisions on my independent visa application.

Now that we understand why the visa was denied, it is time to follow through on our second concern, that of "customer service" and the inconsistent and disgusting behavior of the consulate officers: The Consul General, Mr. Peter Kaestner's letter refers to an "interviewing officer" (paragraph 3, line 5). This is the first problem with the consulate; each time I visited the embassy I spoke with a different officer. Two out of those three officers were rude and impatient. The final officer, may I remind you, verbally abused me, saying she "[would] refuse me, just for the fun of it." When I could not believe my ears, I asked her to repeat what she said, and she confirmed what I feared I had heard. This officer was in Window 5 at noon (Cairo time) on July 21. I could write volumes about this statement, but I will let the officer's ignorant words speak for themselves.

Mr. Kaestner's letter also states that I "could not demonstrate sufficient economic or social ties outside of the U.S…" (paragraph 3, line 6). I presented all the evidence I had of both social and economic ties to the first interviewing officer, neither the second nor the third officers requested that evidence, and if I had presented it to them without their request, I do not even want to imagine what their arrogant and ignorant response would have been. I am attaching a list of ties I have to Egypt.

What irritates me most is how the Department of State/ U.S.C.I.S. interprets the role of family ties as it wishes. They are now considering me a part of my family. When it came time to include me on my parents' green card application (not to be shared outside your office) I was NOT part of the family-- I was AN INDEPENDENT ADULT. Now, when I try to act as an INDEPENDENT ADULT, all of a sudden—I am a part of THE FAMILY. Please have Mr. Kaestner or any fair-minded immigration official explain how you decide when a person is part of their family or not. This is the kind of law, when combined with carelessness and xenophobia that breaks hearts and tears families apart.

Finally, I do not want to hear that this problem is bigger than your office's capabilities. This problem is much bigger than me but I stepped up and asked someone bigger than me to help out— that someone was you. Now I am asking *you* to step up and ask someone bigger than yourselves for help. This is no longer about a visa for me; this has become an issue of human rights. I have NO interest whatsoever in immigrating to the United States after this experience. The only interest I have is that of every human being on this earth, and that is the interest of being with one's family.

Best,
Marwa Helal

Attachments: List of social and economic ties to Egypt

From-from?

Where *am I* from-from? Where are you *from-from*?

SURVEY SAYS:
"You know, I mean your baaackground?" (60 points)
"Oh, but your English is *so* good." (30 points)
"I've always wanted to visit..." (10 points)

DNA Tests for Ethnicity & Genealogical DNA testing |
AncestryDNA

The newest DNA test which helps you find genetic relatives and expand your genealogy research. Order your kit today.

People also ask:
How much is the ancestry DNA kit?
How much does it cost to have a DNA test for ancestry?
What is the cost of ancestry DNA test?
What is the cost of a DNA test?

Amazon.com rating 3.8 (out of 5 stars) 609 reviews

In stock.

The T[---]p Administration Is Making Immigrant Parents Pay $800 for DNA Tests to Get Their Kids Back[8]

---

8 "The T[---]p Administration Is Making Immigrants Parents Pay $800 for DNA Tests to Get Their Kids Back," *GQ Magazine*, Darby, Luke. 11 July 2018.

Green card.

> The green card, which only until recently became green
> again, has a history with a variety of names and colors.
> U.S. Citizenship and Immigration Services (U.S.C.I.S.)
> officially refers to it as the Permanent Resident Card.
> However, it has also been known over time as a Resident
> Alien Card or Alien Registration Receipt Card.[9]

Three years after becoming a citizen I am chatting with my friend
Eman in an Egyptian bakery in Dearborn, Michigan. We are
talking about the upcoming 2016 election and how this will be
the first time I vote. She is telling me about her own journey of
becoming a citizen when she asks rhetorically, "You know that
precarious period while you're waiting for your Green Card, so
you don't leave the country?" I think yes, I know it now. But I left
because I believed myself to be American. Entitled to the right of
return to the place where I was raised and educated. The place
where my family and friends lived. Where my home was.

I am sworn in as a citizen of The United States on a cold day in
March at Cadman Plaza in Brooklyn, New York. Although I know
Cadman Plaza well, having lived near it for the past five years, I
get lost on the way. I arrive late and take a seat in the front row.
The ceremony is mostly American pomp and circumstance. A
summary of the various paths to citizenship. I am sitting next to a
couple of Caribbean young professionals and a very pale Eastern
European woman. I hear the Caribbean man muttering under his
breath. My mood exactly; fellow feeling. The man at the front

9 Citizenpath.com: Immigration Forms Made Simple

of the room is saying something about voting, other privileges of becoming citizens.

We wait over an hour for a judge to swear us in. This is America. This is the America we have been waiting for.

I am not moved. I feel neither the burden nor gift of privilege. I know this country well. I am no newcomer. I was raised here, educated here. I have no illusions about what this is. It has taken me 24 years to gain citizenship and so I do not feel any sense of pride in my "new" country. Portions of my life in it rush through my mind:

Upper Arlington, Ohio a nearly all white suburb where on the first day, my fifth grade teacher Mrs. Bachman, made sure to put me in the care of my Indian-American and Turkish-American friends, Alka and Eda.

Albquerque, New Mexico. The first place I felt safe in my skin.

The final move of my adolescence—Ludington, Michigan, a rural town on the western shore of Lake Michigan—deemed me numb. Making books and nature my best friends. There were many other moves, but these are the important ones.

Finally, they call each of us up to receive our citizenship certificates. It feels much like receiving "perfect attendance" awards in elementary school. Some people have adorned themselves. Some are very old. Some are in traditional African and Asian wear. One man still has the maker's tag on the sleeve of his blazer. One woman hasn't removed the stitches from the vent of her skirt. I feel sadness at their effort. Most of them are Black and old. Some with canes. We—migrants, skilled workers, artists, refugees, asylum seekers, mothers, brothers, fathers, sisters. Effort for what? Pride for whom?

A country that ensures we are harassed for being whoever we are presumed to be and never who we actually are. A country that shoots Black and brown boys, girls, women and men in the back, in the chest, in their cars, in front of their children. A country that deals in drones. A country that has no trouble trading blood for oil. A country that intervenes only when it is convenient for its own interests. A country that fakes left but passes a hard right.

Maybe I want to feel whatever it is they feel. Whatever made them take pride in themselves on this day. But I don't.

The bulletproof windows—you can see but not feel through.

The consulate officers with their broken Arabic. The boys that barely got high school degrees playing border officer, G.I. Joe and super trooper. Don't get me started on TSA. The fingerprint machines. The ones born here claiming they ain't immigrants. That somehow they're more native than a Native. The ones that believe they work harder than Black people and that's why they've got what they've got. Nah, America. My citizenship is so I can say: GO BACK WHERE *YOU* CAME FROM.[10] I'm from here. Where are you *from-from*?

In loving memory, my struggle for citizenship: 1983-2013

---

10 "I love America more than any other country in this world, and, exactly for this reason, I insist on the right to criticize her perpetually." James A. Baldwin from *Notes of a Native Son*, 1955.

Hatem. That's my middle-brother. He aged out, too. He now lives in the United Kingdom. I encouraged him to leave. I was angry and bitter. I wanted the best for him and still do.

I miss him now that I'm back here.

He stood by the garage door, waving at me when I left for Egypt. I didn't know then that I wouldn't see him again for another year and a half.

When he started going to school with me, I was in the second grade. I would give him the window seat on the bus so that he could fall asleep. Otherwise, he'd suffer from motion sickness.

I.N.S.: Immigration and Naturalization Services is the former name of what we now know as U.S. Citizenship and Immigration Services (U.S.C.I.S)—a component of the United States Department of Homeland Security.

Naturalization.

Definition[11] of naturalize:

[nach-er-uh-lahyz, nach-ruh-]

verb (used with object), naturalized, naturalizing.

1. to confer upon (an alien) the rights and privileges of a citizen.
2. to introduce (organisms) into a region and cause them to flourish as if native.

11 "What does *Webster's* say about soul?" Gil Scott-Heron, "Comment No.1," *Small Talk at 125th and Lenox* © 1970.

$\int$-2. The visa my father was granted in 1983 when he came to the U.S. on an AMIDEAST Fellowship. My mother, Hatem and I were listed as dependents on that visa when we accompanied him. The terms of this visa required my father to return to Egypt for two years after his studies.

My parents had every intention of returning but they didn't want to disrupt our education. My father made many attempts to fulfill the requirement. One time taking my youngest brother, Yaser, with him to Egypt. Our family split between Egypt and Ohio. But he couldn't stand the distance. He called my mother crying. Often. A fact they don't share with me until I'm much older.

We stayed legal.

I turned 21 a few months before my father completed this requirement.

I also turned 21 a few months before the Child Status Protection Act was amended to immigration law on August 6, 2002[12]. This is the only law that exists to protect children from the consequences of the immigration system. It means those who meet the requirements have a chance not to be forced to leave their homes, families, schools and communities (read: deported) based on a decision they did not make.

---

1 2 Child Status Protection Act (CSPA) amended the Immigration Nationality Act (INA) by changing who qualifies as a child for purposes of immigrant. This law permits certain beneficiaries (see the glossary for a definition of the term "beneficiary") to retain classification as a "child," even if he or she has reached the age of 2 1.

Kenyatta—is the U.S. Vice Consul who grants my green card in 2007. Nearly three years after the first time I stepped up to Window 7, I was back. And I was nervous. And the first thing he said was: "It looks like you're going back home."

Later, I will write him a thank you letter.[13]

As I'm leaving the embassy this time, I notice a family, a couple in their mid-30s with two children in tow. They've been rejected. Though they've received lottery visas, they've been turned away. The father returns to the window just like I had that summer of 2005. He wants to understand. Why?

13   See: Epilogue.

Laura Bush, First Lady of the U.S. is on television. She is posing with Egyptian schoolgirls in front of the pyramids.

I sneer back at the television, wishing her fake smile would melt in the desert heat like Soundgarden's "Black Hole Sun" music video.

This is made worse by the fact that I am waiting for a call from Congressman Pete Hoekstra's Chief of Staff, Amy Plaster.[14] I have 180 days to figure out how I'm going to stay in the U.S. and my dad thinks she can help.

All I remember from that conversation is yelling:

"I don't want to hear any of this legal garbage about 'home-country.'"[15]

14 The first time I meet Amy Plaster it's in her polished Capitol building office a few weeks before we have this telephone conversation. At the end of the meeting, where it's clear she can't do anything for me and my family, she asks me where I like to eat in D.C. I recognize my response to that question as anxiety now. Dry mouth. A loss for words. Staring through her. Looking for ways out. Anxiety: a neat white people word for rage. Justifiable rage.

15 Home country definition: the country in which a person was born [and usually raised], regardless of the present country of residence and citizenship.

Mistaken for:

Brazilian at a McDonald's in Cairo;

Colombian in Brazil;

Native-American at a soccer game in Ludington, Michigan;

I----li at a Tim Horton's in Delaware, Ohio;

Sri Lankan in a classroom in New York City;

Dominican;

Greek;

Italian;

Indian;

Iranian, Malaysian, Mexican;

Pakistani, Puerto Rican;

Spanish, etc.[16]

---

16 I'd like to take this moment to apologize to all the people who ask me
   for directions in various languages. On train platforms, in airports, in
   stores (no, I do not work here) and mostly on streets. The ones I stop
   for and the ones I don't. I see how frustrating it is for you when it turns
   out I don't speak your language. It frustrates me, too.

Nine/11 isn't to blame. The underlying racism and neglect in the immigration system was always there. It just made it worse. We are still living out the consequences. And more[17].

17 "Everything that was, is more: brutality, injustice, poverty, anger; but also clarity, knowledge, understanding and, possibly, determination." Ahdaf Soueif, "Egypt's revolution won't be undone: the people still have the will." *The Guardian*. 30 May 2014.

"One-800-IMMIGRATION. Payment Plans. Free Consultation."

That's what it says on the advertisement above the person sitting across from me on the train. Jon Roland (compensated spokesperson) mimics concern. The creases around his eyes and wrinkles in his forehead say so. But he is an old, white man. It's not his age or skin color that betray him, it is his false smile.

I wonder how much they spent on this advertisement. If it is more or less than what the attorney, who would have taken on my case as an asylum seeker, would have charged. Probably more, I decide. The attorney was a Native American woman in the Detroit area accustomed to doing pro-bono work.

> "I can't even begin to picture how we would deport 11 million people in a few years where we don't have a police state, where the police can't break down your door at will and take you away without a warrant," said Michael Chertoff, who led a significant increase in immigration enforcement as the secretary of Homeland Security under President George W. Bush.
>
> Finding those immigrants would be difficult, experts said. Police officers across the country would need to ask people for proof of residency or citizenship during traffic stops and street encounters. The Border Patrol would need highway checkpoints across the Southwest and near the Canadian border. To avoid racial profiling, any American could expect to be stopped and asked for papers.
>
> ...
>
> [ICE Director] said mass deportations would add chaos to a dysfunctional immigration system.
>
> ...

Mr. T[---]p has promised that the wall will be big, beautiful, tall and strong. Spanning 1,000 miles along the southern border, it will stem the flow of immigrants bringing drugs and crime. And, yes, Mexico will pay for the Great Wall of T[---]p, as he has called it."[18]

18 "What Would It Take for Donald T[---]p to Deport 11 Million and Build a Wall?" *The New York Times*. Preston, Julia; Rappeport, Alan and Richter, Matt. 19 May 2016.

$\mathbb{P}$ermanent Resident[19], that's what I was before I became a citizen.

Getting Help

If you need advice, see the Finding Legal Advice webpage. You may contact the U.S.C.I.S. District Office near your home for a list of organizations that may be able to assist you in preparing your application.

Versions of Green Card That Are No Longer Valid

If you have a previous version of the alien registration card (e.g., USCIS Form AR-3, Form AR-103 or Form I-151), you must replace it with a current green card.

What the Law Says

Section 264 of the Immigration and Nationality Act (INA) states, "Every alien in the United States… shall be issued a certificate of alien registration or an alien registration receipt card in such form and manner and at such time as shall be prescribed under regulations…." It also says, "Every alien, eighteen years of age and over, shall at all times carry with him and have in his personal possession any certificate of alien registration or alien registration receipt card issued to him…. Any alien who fails to comply with [these provisions] shall be guilty of a misdemeanor…" The specific requirements and procedures for applying to renew an expiring green card are contained in the Code of Federal Regulations [CFR] at 8 CFR section 264.5.[20]

---

19   … or "green card," is a plastic card with the individual's biographic information, photo, fingerprint, and expiration date issued by U.S. Citizenship and Immigration Services. It authorizes the green card holder the right to live and work in the United States indefinitely.

20   "Getting Help, Versions of Green Card That Are No Longer Valid, and What the Law Says." text from USCIS.gov

(Q)uestion: How many American border patrol officers did it take to fingerprint me when I landed in the U.S. in December of 2007? Answer: Three.

In other words: Two too many.[21]

First, there was some confusion over which finger it was they were supposed to be printing.

No, wait—*first*, they called me "Marla...."

I come back to the U.S. because it is what I know. Because this is where my family and friends are. Where my home is. Where my work is. I come back because I am American. It is hard because Egypt is where my family and friends are. Where my home is. Where my work is. It is hard because I am Egyptian.

I land with my mother who accompanied me on the return flight after a brutal layover in Charles De-Gaulle airport where two French security agents treat us like we aren't worthy of their French airport soil and banish us to the ice cold terminal reserved for non-Westerners; non- 'good' passport holders.[22]

At customs in the U.S., I see myself in a young girl of maybe 11 or 12 years old. Tall for her age, as I had been. Her hair neatly pulled back with a side part, like mine. Her posture slumped in

---

21   Homeland Security Jobs: The Department of Homeland Security has unique career opportunities that will challenge your mind and reward your skills and talents. As a Homeland Security employee, you will help secure our borders, airports, seaports, and waterways; research and develop the latest security technologies; respond to natural disasters or terrorist acts; and analyze intelligence reports. More at: dhs.gov/topic/homeland-security-jobs

22   Note: The security agents, one French-Tunisian and the other French-Mauritanian, teach my mom and me about Arab-on-Arab racism that night in France. Their message is clear. If you are not of the Francophone Arab countries, you do not belong.

the direction of her attention. She has politely distanced herself from her family; her father and mother are in a tired frenzy over their open luggage on the security conveyer belt. The customs agent is asking her mom about the contents of the luggage. She has found: lib. Lib Abyad, toasted pumpkin seeds.

Confiscated, an invasive species.

The girl watches her family from about six feet away near the glass doors marking the border and the next security check. It is her calm observational demeanor I recognize in myself. This balancing act of being here and not here. Being of this place and not of it. Being visible and invisible. Are we on the outside looking in? Or on the inside looking out?

Returning to Egypt is hard and doesn't happen often enough. But when I see Cairo from the airplane window… the plane becomes land and Cairo, the sky.

I remember the aerial view before the Sahara was developed into the lush green it is today. Desert. Spacious. I remember the Malaysian student sitting in the middle seat the last time I was back. Her breath reeked like that of someone who had been traveling for days as she leaned over me to see out the window, but I did not pull my head away from her or the window. The laws of personal space are null when you're on Egypt Air. She tells me she is beginning a new school year at Al Mansurah University and boasts of their science departments. This is the same university where my mother and father met.

Every time I see my parents while I am in Cairo they seem ages older. I am not used to this much time passing between visits. Six months. Eight months. Nine months in between. The time between visits grows in correlation with my stability in Egypt.

I am at the airport saying goodbye to them that summer I failed at the embassy. They are going back to the U.S. after changing their flights, extending their stay as much as possible. It hits me: I am stuck indefinitely in Egypt. They are rolling their suitcases to security when I collapse like a child. A 24-year-old child. My aunt holds me. My head buried in her body. I black out. I do not know how I get to my cousin's house. I sleep for what seems like two weeks. From my bed, I overhear my auntie, talking to the other on the phone, "She shouldn't be alone, she shouldn't be alone." I drift back to sleep.[23]

23   New: ProPublica has obtained audio from inside a U.S. Customs and Border Protection facility, in which children can be heard wailing.

Border Patrol agent jokes, "We have an orchestra here."

The children on the recording are between four and 10 years old.

Listen to Children Who've Just Been Separated from Their Parents at the Border—ProPublica (propublica.org). Source: Twitter 6/18/18 3:53 pm

"We cannot allow all of these people to invade our Country. When somebody comes in, we must immediately, with no Judges or Court Cases, bring them back from where they came. Our system is a mockery to good immigration policy and Law and Order. Most children come without parents...." @therealD[----]dT[---]p": Twitter 6/24/18 11:02 am

DNR adds to list of unwanted aquatic invasive species

The Department of Natural Resources recently announced the addition of seven species to Michigan's prohibited species list of aquatic invasive species. An additional species already on the list was also modified from a prohibited species to a restricted species.

Any species considered for listing as prohibited or restricted must be not native to Michigan. Prohibited species generally are not present or are in very limited areas, whereas restricted species are generally widespread and naturalized within the state.

The decision came during the Nov. 6 meeting of the Natural Resources Commission, where DNR Director Keith Creagh signed Invasive Species Order Amendment No. 1 of 2014.

Prior to this order there were 33 aquatic species listed as prohibited or restricted. The following species were added to the prohibited species list:

• Stone moroko – part of the minnow family, this species is a known carrier of a parasite that can negatively impact other fishes.

• Zander – a close relative of the walleye, this species could compete with the native fish or reproduce with it and create a hybrid.

• Wels catfish – this fish is considered a serious danger to native fish populations.

• Killer shrimp – this species is an aggressive predator and could severely threaten the trophic levels of the Great Lakes

by preying on a range of invertebrates.

• Yabby – this large crayfish would negatively impact other crayfish species.

• Golden mussel – similar to zebra and quagga mussels, this species has destructive qualities that would threaten native biodiversity.

• Red swamp crayfish – this species can quickly dominate waterbodies and is virtually impossible to eradicate.

Additionally, rusty crayfish were moved from prohibited to restricted classification to allow for their limited possession for the purpose of destroying them for consumption, fertilizer or trash. This species already is widespread throughout the state, yet regulations previously didn't allow for the collection of them for consumptive purposes.

"Crayfish trapping is a growing activity in Michigan and allowing our anglers to enjoy some tablefare while assisting to remove an invasive species is a win/win," said Nick Popoff, Aquatic Species and Regulatory Affairs manager for the DNR.

This order comes following a meeting of the governors of each of the Great Lakes states committing to blocking the spread of 16 "least wanted" aquatic invasive species through prohibitions and restrictions. Nine of the 16 already were prohibited in

Michigan under the Natural Resources and Environmental Protection Act; six more were designated as prohibited with the signing of this order. Please note, the remaining "least wanted" aquatic invasive species is a plant. The Michigan Department of Agriculture and Rural Development has authority over plants and is expected to add water soldier as a prohibited species through the Commission of Agriculture and Rural Development in January.

For more information on Michigan's fight against aquatic invasive species, visit www.michigan.gov/invasivespecies.

Michigan state parks accepting applications for 2015 campground hosts

Each year during the warmer months, hundreds of volunteers spend their summers camping for free at Michigan state parks and state forest campgrounds in exchange for their service as campground hosts. Although the 2015 camping season is still several months away, the Department of Natural Resources is accepting campground host applications now, with positions available as early as April and as late as October.

Campground hosts are responsible for 30 hours of service per week, including directing visitors to their campsites, answering questions about the park or recreation area, planning

campground activities and performing light park maintenance duties. Volunteer duties take place throughout the summer (including weekends and holidays), with a minimum commitment of four consecutive weeks.

New campground hosts are required to attend training, which will take place June 3-4, at the Ralph A. MacMullan Center in Roscommon, Mich.

For additional information about the DNR's Campground Host Program and how to apply, go to www.michigan.gov/dnrvolunteers or contact Miguel Rodriguez at 517-284-6127.

SOURCE: *Ludington Daily News*, 10 November 2014.

Special registration is a [tracking] system for certain non-citizens within the United States, initiated in September 2002 as part of the War on Terrorism. This system has two separate portions: port-of-entry registration and domestic registration. In each case, the registrant is required to be fingerprinted, photographed, and interrogated. In addition, they are required to provide detailed information about their plans and updates to the U.S. Immigration and Customs Enforcement (ICE) in case of changes of plans. Travel to and from the U.S. is limited to certain ports only.

This procedure is required of males over the age of sixteen who entered the United States legally on particular types of visa (primarily student, work, and tourist) from certain countries. Four groups of countries have been announced:

- Group 1: Iran, Iraq, Libya, Sudan or Syria
- Group 2: Afghanistan, Algeria, Bahrain, Eritrea, Lebanon, Morocco, North Korea, Oman, Qatar, Somalia, Tunisia, the United Arab Emirates, Yemen
- Group 3: Pakistan, Saudi Arabia
- Group 4: Bangladesh, Egypt, Indonesia, Jordan, Kuwait

Brazil was eventually added to this list.

In retaliation, Brazil implemented a similar policy on January 1, 2004.

On January 14, 2004 American Airlines pilot Dale Robin Hirsch was detained in Brazil for raising his middle finger while undergoing the new Brazilian security measures.[24]

---

24 "Brazil detains U.S. airline crew after pilot makes obscene gesture." 14 Jan 2004. CNN.com. 29 Apr 2010.

I remember the repeated e-mails, all-caps subject line, from our International Student Office at Ohio Wesleyan asking applicable international students to register.

My brother and friends in white vans.

Large 12-15 passenger white vans, just like the ones they disappear Arab men in. Picked up and taken in for questioning. The lucky ones released, the unlucky: hauled off to CIA black sites. I overhear one of my dad's friends, one I call 3mo, tell him about how it happened to his brother in Florida.

The United States of America is:

a) beautiful;
b) complicated;
c) in recent years, coloring books for grownups have been on the rise—a remedy for the high level of stress many adults are living with.

Victorious. "Marwa is victorious," was my Facebook status after I walked out of the U.S. Embassy in Cairo on October 29, 2007.

I am 26 when my 180-day-dilemma turned 912.5 [25] begins to end. And a new dilemma begins.

We talk about who has smoked what and when as we pass the apple shishah around on the rooftop. The Brooklyn Museum looks like Washington, D.C. from up here and the sun already sets in Manhattan. Our discussion: a study of the sunlight. We consider how the light has aged since the time it left the sun. As if it were suddenly tangible.

Tomorrow, I will be on a plane to Cairo and I will see a prism in the thick rounded corners of the window and remember this conversation. But I haven't packed yet. It was the same way when I was leaving Egypt. Pacing between the balcony and my bedroom. Stepping around or over the open suitcases but never putting anything inside.

At least I have words for what I could never carry. Though what are words but an attempt to replicate thoughts, dreams, events and memory? And what am I but a word without context? How do I tell a story in this language when I exist in another? When you move as much as I have, you learn sometimes the emptiest thing is an overstuffed suitcase.

25   nearly 1,001 nights for any Orientalists reading this

"…I saw one of my girlfriends in my dreams before I met her," Benicio says. I offer to interpret another—his twin, Jericho, tells me he dreamt of a parrot flying around his aunt's house where he was going to make a phone call. I tell him the parrot represents freedom and the phone represents positive communication. I ask him what he thinks his aunt represents. He says he hasn't seen her in a long time. The silence falls naturally as the shuttle rattles by. We turn away from each other to watch the sunset.

The dilemma of my disorientation is this: sometimes. When I'm driving through the tunnel on Geary Boulevard—under Masonic Avenue—I look at the fluorescent lights overhead and feel sure that I'll find Cairo on the other side. I step hard on the gas like a child who believes she can dig her way to China. There is this uncertain certainty that when I come out of the tunnel's neon shadows I will be there. On Shari' Omar Ibn il Khattab, meters away from the Midan il Gami' market and the cream-colored balconies of il Korba. The vision is so convincing, I feel I will find things exactly as I left them.

My eyes adjust to the light outside the tunnel. I hear a car behind me honking to pass. I make a right. A pair of officers, dressed in summer white uniforms stand, wilting in the heat. Under awnings, skinny-wrists wipe the latest layer of dust off store windows with pieces of crumpled newspaper.

The baker is shuffling puffs of wheat bread on the blackened shelf of a fiery oven with a wooden paddle. A line of people wait for their yellow bags of bread, a veiled woman holds a smudged baby. She's selling tissues for 25 piastres a piece.

I pass a tiny Fiat, a newer Toyota and a rusty black and white taxi.

Changing lanes,
I realize

I'm almost home.

White men from places like Germany, Norway or Switzerland get U.S. visas and green cards expedited 99 percent faster than the average applicant[26].

What I know is, I had applied for the green card lottery twice before. The lottery opens in fall, which means I was always really dark from the summers in the sun when I took my photo for the application. When I applied from Egypt, my picture had been retouched in a studio in Helipolis, Masr il Gedida, my skin lightened and my lips pinked.

The only children being sworn in for citizenship with me: little white, blonde kids, whose parents were courted by rich multinational companies to immigrate, all travel and legal expenses paid. Not the briefcase of rejections and notifications of missing applications my parents hide under the bookcase in the basement. Not the sleepless nights, months and years waiting for responses, thousands spent on immigration lawyers who already know we are a lost cause.

26 I made this one up. Yes, I'm angry and suspicious. Of a country that made us pay taxes but made sure we could never vote, never belong, never feel safe and always kept us on the outside. And still.

I wrote this statement about Norway YEARS before T---p's statement in January 2018. Thanks for confirming it, Shithole.

It is the X in Brexit. And T---p's dream of a wall.

- **X** Living in a post-factual society make believing we are a post-racial one.
- **X** A veiled woman being pushed into oncoming traffic.
- **X** Sikh mistaken for Muslim out of imaginary fear.
- **X** The billions spent on America's war machine.
- **X** Xenophobia, it ought to be a diagnosable disease.

...Y our land/ ... is my land/ From California, to the New York island
From the redwood forest/ to the Gulf Stream waters/
This land was made for you and Me... [27]

27 *... In the shadow of the steeple I saw my people, By the relief office I seen my people; As they stood there hungry, I stood there asking Is this land made for you and me?* lyrics by Woodie Guthrie, "This Land is Your Land," copyright 1956.

Zoom in. Zoom out.

Look. I'm trying to show you something.

Ecology, 91(10), 2010, pp. 2965–2974
© 2010 by the Ecological Society of America

Native fish diversity alters the effects of an invasive species on food webs

Michael P. Carey[1] and David H. Wahl

*Illinois Natural History Survey and Program in Ecology, Evolution, and Conservation Biology, University of Illinois,
1816 South Oak Street, Champaign, Illinois 61820 USA*

Abstract. Aquatic communities have been altered by invasive species, with impacts on native biodiversity and ecosystem function. At the same time, native biodiversity may mitigate the effects of an invader. Common carp (*Cyprinus carpio*) is a ubiquitous, invasive fish species that strongly influences community and ecosystem processes. We used common carp to test whether the potential effects of an invasive species are altered across a range of species diversity in native communities. In mesocosms, treatments of zero, one, three, and six native fish species were used to represent the nested subset patterns observed in fish communities of lakes in Illinois, USA. The effect of the invader was tested across fish richness treatments by adding common carp to the native community and substituting native biomass with common carp. Native species and intraspecific effects reduced invader growth. The invader reduced native fish growth; however, the negative effect was minimized with increasing native richness. The zooplankton grazer community was modified by a top-down effect from the invader that increased the amount of phytoplankton. Neither the invader nor richness treatments influenced total phosphorus or community metabolism. Overall, the invader reduced resources for native species, and the effect scaled with how the invader was incorporated into the community. Higher native diversity mitigated the impact of the invader, confirming the need to consider biodiversity when predicting the impacts of invasive species.

Key words: biodiversity; common carp; Cyprinus carpio; *food webs; Illinois, USA; invasion; invasive species.*

EPILOGUE

SUBJECT: *Thank You*

    Tue, Jul 1, 2008 at 2:12 PM

  To: Kenyatta--@state.gov

Dear Mr. Kenyatta,

I doubt you will remember me, but I met you this past summer at the U.S. Consulate in Cairo when you issued me a Diversity-Visa. I was the one who asked for your card so that I could eventually e-mail you this note. I was working at *Egypt Today* magazine, had graduated from a university in the U.S. and had started my journalism career here, and so you joked, I was asking for your card so I could get in touch about an interview for CNN. (Perhaps that rings a bell?) From your perspective, "[I] was going home," a sentiment that meant a lot to me—that an American saw it that way.

Now, I realize you're not completely responsible for granting the visa to me. However, I wanted to thank you for your cordial manner during the interview. My previous experience at the consulate had been unpleasant. I had been mistreated by a consulate officer who told me she would, "refuse me for the fun of it," and proceeded to do just that. I realize that the cruelty she displayed is probably part of your training. But I found her behavior unjustified and later filed a complaint.

The repercussions of her denying me the visa were painful, and came as a final, stunning blow in a long-line of disappointments in dealing with the U.S. immigration system. Though [her decision] also gave me the opportunity to get to know my country, my family, and become re-Egyptianized, I was also forced to live far from my immediate family.

Needless to say, after that experience, I was nervous and fearful when I approached your window. I can't tell you how much I appreciated your warmth during our conversation, and how that interaction reinstilled some of my hope in the system.

I hope you're well and still running things in Cairo.

Warm salaams from the U.S.,
Marwa Helal

EPIEPILOGUE

Brooklyn, New York
March 15, 2018

I have told you the story of losing a country twice.

I've told you some secrets, played you my songs, and so we are friends now. Some of you I consider family. And like any good kin, you may have some follow up questions. You can always tell when someone is holding back or not telling the whole story—out of shame, shyness, or that it's just too much.

It's just too much. This book is just the beginning of what I have left to unpack.

There is some shame, too and tiredness. Tired of working so hard to prove my worth to a country that has yet to see me, and us. Tired of fighting myself on how to tell this story without betraying myself. Every trope is a trap. Even the one you write yourself.

Though I am a few weeks away from turning 37 as I write this, sometimes I am still that child asking my parents: *When are we going back?* I have been missing home my entire life.

To say that the immigration system has marked or defined me would be an understatement.

And those brief years in Egypt, they were the most formative of my life. I fell in love, the real kind. And I risked or lost that love in my choice to return. It didn't survive the distance. It didn't survive who I asked myself to become in my choice to return. But parts of that love survive in these poems.

Both of my grandmothers pass away shortly after I return. I am grateful to have had that time with them and to have known their warmth and experienced the light and pure understanding of their eyes.

I return because of the green card lottery. Or, I return because at my most heartbroken, I made a deal with god: *if* I returned, I would tell this story. I would tell it for myself, for my family, and all the families separated or turned away because of a broken and racist immigration system.

Homeland security's terms: 'legal' or 'illegal.' Both end up with many of the same consequences: soul loss, loss of familial ties, and in some cases, loss of native culture and language. Both terms inherently deny the immigrant's humanity.

So I made my own term: I, Invasive species.

Now that I've told you my story, I can truly begin returning now. There will still be mornings when I wake up and think I am in Egypt, but that's okay. Because the America I return to is not the America I left.

The America I return to is the one we are making together.

The America I return to is part of a world that is becoming more aware of how we are inextricably connected. We are each other and complicit in these systems. Racism isn't just an American problem. It is prevalent in every one of our cultures and countries. In fact, we bring it with us as much as we find it here. Refugees are treated with disdain and fear; treated like burdens the world over. I saw with my own eyes how in Egypt, Sudanese refugees were treated poorly. Now Syrian and Yemeni refugees struggle to find refuge there. And to write a whole book and not speak of how the Egyptian government is not only complicit in the oppression of its own people, but of our Palestinian brothers and sisters, would be hypocrisy.

In the years since my return, the immigration industrial complex has become more aggressive, more racist, more abusive and more expensive. The formation of ICE; massive deportations; freezing cells; threats of a border wall; threats to end the diversity green card lottery and temporary protected status; and asylum is harder than ever to get.

And it's from here, as I finish a much earlier draft of what you just read, that I watch the small protests I used to partake in become a revolution in Egypt. It is my country's incredible history and the spirit of its people I invoke.

Each of us must work to undo these systems.

In this sense, the world is one country.

Otherwise, what are we all doing? Who are we asking ourselves to become?

I still have a few more songs to play for you.

III.

i am made to leave i am made to return

Once you drink from the Nile, you are destined to return.

Egyptian proverb

heathrow is my favorite

at customs i am met by an agent who looks like rumi. turban, beard, mustache and all, see >> it is nearly 7am when we land in london, (middle of the night in the states) and i havent slept on the flight >> in my groggy state when rumi-agent asks *what kind of writing* i do (i wrote writer-editor as my occupation on the landing card) i tell him *i used to be a journalist but now im a poet* because i believe he is rumi i think this will impress him >> then he asks *what kind of poems* i write >> and i give him this look like: *we both know what kind of poems i write...* followed by a *look at the two of us here talking poetry*

at customs >> and he nods and i play along and say: *all sorts* >> and he gives me his approval > a twinkle in his eye > a blessing—he stamps my passport and says: *very good* >> i flash my eyebrows < smile < say *thank you* and am on my way <<<<

generation of feeling

these growing pains though
this good will hunting
we
fallen twigs
look like bones
waiting to be lit

i am trying to tell you something about how
rearranging words
rearranges the universe

dream that wrote me

ive been assigned to be the googlestreetview photographer for the countryside of the delta region in egypt. this is where my mother's side of the family is from. it's my favorite part of the world. still largely untouched by 'civilization.' im driving down an unpaved road alone. the car im in is a dusty clunker and i have the windows open just enough to get some air while keeping the dirt from the road out.

im filled with bliss at the first sight of the green crop fields, their perfect lines, rows of irrigation flowing between them. i get out of the car to snap a picture. i take my phone out to take a selfie, but before i get a chance to flip the camera lens toward me, a horse appears on the screen. he is a beautiful tan horse, very friendly with a white strip down the front of his nose and he nuzzles my hand that is holding the phone.

next, i realize i need to go to the bathroom (i actually needed to pee in waking life) so the horse and i walk to an outhouse. it is a metal shanty marked with a "women" sign. it is dark inside.

i sense the first stall is occupied so i move to the second one. the person in there hasnt bothered to pull the curtain over their stall and i notice it is muhammad ali. i try to hide the shock on my face. he is sitting on the pot, drinking out of a large bottle of liquor. he tells me not to tell anyone that ive seen him like this then takes another swig.

returning note no. 1

your wait time will be approximately: 90 minutes
your wait time will be approximately: 92 minutes
your wait time will be approximately: 93 minutes

leaving note no. 2

oceanic feeling
corporeal memory

i am writing a scene:

we are driving to sinai. remind me—how would you describe how you taught me to manage those deep mountainous curves? i remember it being counterintuitive, to coast when i wanted to brake and to give it gas while we were within the tightest curve of curve.

flo sends sinai instruction:

„to coast" sounds great - slow down before the curve begins, stop breaking as the curve begins, hold that speed (= or coast) during the first part of the curve (ideally at maximum speed that won't hurl you off the street) until you reach the apex and then... wrooom, whiplash. :)

I really really love to remember that trip (and i'm sorry you had to change your tires after it) - just a month ago i sorted the picture of these days full of wistfulness (in addition to that: you must have been mind reading—last week i felt so grateful for having met you (that was triggered less so by memory, but more so by all those things you have shown me without knowing...

leaving note no. 3

i ocean you

returning note no. 5

ive grown tired of keeping a safe distance

of ritual

somewhere far within ocean not steelpan but steelpan's cousin
makes me feel warm and distant i want it to stop raining making
a watermark black and panther shape on my shoe i want someone
to pay me to be me just pay me to be free i am tired of everyone
telling me also thinking i am sweet when all i want is to lick his
salty neck when they ask me to account for my time on earth i
will come with an account of the number of times i licked his
salty neck confess my bitterness at those who wrote and spoke but
never did act my bitterness for falsehood and failure to confront
them, it, them it is difficult to write about sex at a time when men
are failing our men are failing us

    but i can write you of ritual of ritual of ritual a structure of
feeling a problematic repetition you see i am trying to break the
mold i have no form rumi wrote: my place is placeless a trace of
the traceless remember the ones who were there for you put the
sound machine on like ███████ playing for a bird maybe ill get paid
tonight maybe ill get laid tonight maybe i am one of them

    in the ocean

    call it a city that never sleeps but never have seen my cairo its
bridges its whirring lit and whirring blurring everyone here has a
car and a line of credit this is capitalism's gift and globalization is
new because we finally gave it a name and now my uncle is buying
persimmons from the lady on the corner where she sits and peels
and cores zucchini and bamya for cooking for cooking

returning note no. 6

when you know youre walking into a memory before youve
made it

returning note no. 7

what did you dream?
that he was little and cute,
wanting to tell me stories
i was visiting you

returning note no. 10

q: i find that even the most mediocre photos i took in egypt are more beautiful than anything i actually put effort into shooting here. is there a word for that?

a: roo7.

the middle east[1] is not only missing it has a serious problem

what im trying to say is that saying "north africa" isnt like saying "north america" or "south america." north africa is not a separate continent. separate from africa. if you buy into this ideology and its byproducts: SWANA, MENA, the middle east, and whatever else they might want to call this region, then you are partaking in white ideology and its byproduct: all oppressive systems. i have very distinct memories of being in undergrad international studies seminars and getting into arguments with my fellow africans who insisted that north africa is not part of africa. and why is that, hmm? isnt it for the same reason they divide everything? what am i trying to show you? where have they put all of the airports? their "tourist" destinations? who does their bidding? where have they spread their "democracy?" who gets the most foreign aid in the region? the beginnings of an essay? one question we all know the answer to: who is they? make sure youre not they today...nor tomorrow. in this sense, the 'middle east' is not only missing, it has a serious problem: its complicity in oppressing black and palestinian people. this isnt to dismiss or diminish the oppression of the peoples of the middle east but to say no revolution can succeed without confronting this reality.

1   Middle East, the lands around the southern and eastern shores of the Mediterranean Sea, extending from Morocco to the Arabian Peninsula and Iran and, by some definitions, sometimes beyond. The central part of this general area was formerly called the Near East, a name given to it by some of the first modern Western geographers and historians, who tended to divide what they called the Orient into three regions. Near East applied to the region nearest Europe, extending from the Mediterranean Sea to the Persian Gulf; Middle East, from the Persian Gulf to Southeast Asia; and Far East, those regions facing the Pacific Ocean.

The change in usage began to evolve prior to World War II and tended to be confirmed during that war, when the term Middle East was given to the British military command in Egypt. By the mid-20th century a common definition of the Middle East encompassed the states or territories of Turkey, Cyprus, Syria, Lebanon, Iraq, Iran, I[----]l, the West Bank, the Gaza Strip, Jordan, Egypt, Sudan, Libya, and the various states and territories of Arabia proper (Saudi Arabia, Kuwait, Yemen, Oman, Bahrain, Qatar, and the Trucial States, or Trucial Oman [now United Arab Emirates]). Subsequent events have tended, in loose usage, to enlarge the number of lands included in the definition. The three North African countries of Tunisia, Algeria, and Morocco are closely connected in sentiment and foreign policy with the Arab states. In addition, geographic factors often require statesmen and others to take account of Afghanistan and Pakistan in connection with the affairs of the Middle East.

Occasionally, Greece is included in the compass of the Middle East because the Middle Eastern (then Near Eastern) question in its modern form first became apparent when the Greeks rose in rebellion to assert their independence of the Ottoman Empire in 1821 (see Eastern Question). Turkey and Greece, together with the predominantly Arabic-speaking lands around the eastern end of the Mediterranean, were also formerly known as the Levant.

Use of the term Middle East nonetheless remains unsettled, and some agencies (notably the United States State Department and certain bodies of the United Nations) still employ the term Near East. Source: Encyclopedia Britannica. Web. 3.16.18.

if this was a different kind of story id tell you about the sea

if this was a different kind of story id tell you about the sea
if this was a *different kind of story id tell you about the sea*
*if this was a diff*erent kind of story id tell you about the sea
if this was a different kind of story id *tell you about* the sea
if this was a different kind of story id tell you about the sea
if this was a different *kind of story id* tell you about the sea
if this was a different kind of story id *tell you about* the sea
if this was a different kind of story id tell you about the sea
if this was a different kind of story id tell you about the sea
if this *was a different kind* of story id tell you about the sea
if this was a different kind of story id tell you about the sea
if this was a different kind of story id tell you about the sea
if this was a different kind of story *id tell you about the* sea
if this was a different kind of story id tell you about the sea
if this was a different kind of story id tell you about the sea
if this was a different kind of story id tell you about the sea
if this was a different kind of story id tell you about the sea
if this was a different kind of story id tell you about the sea
if this was a different kind of story id tell you about the sea
if this was a different kind of story id tell you about the sea
if this was a different kind of story id tell you about the sea
if this was a *different kind of story* id tell you about the sea
if this was a different *kind of story id tell you about the* sea
if this was a different kind of story id tell you about the sea
if this was a different kind of story id tell you about the sea
if this was a different kind of story id tell you about the sea
if this was a different kind of story id tell you about the sea
if this was a different kind of story id tell you about the sea
if this was a different kind of story id tell you about the sea

ghost purchase

by #05661

> i could buy these reading cups: now worth
> between 3,000 and 5,000 francs. i'd go to
> galleries in algeria or tunisia, i'd have them
> removed from the cabinets in the museums,
> from beneath the dust, i'd make the transaction,
> they could belong to me then and there. i
> even thought of buying them with the money i
> would make from this poem. i even thought of
> including them in this poem, but as i progress,
> they become more distant, and who needs
> reading cups when there is a poem to be read i
> mean written. the cups once bought would lose
> value like most of life a diminishing return or
> rather, latent; ghost.

about #05661

refugee 05661 arrived at the island of Algiers when she was
12-years-old and lived in the southern united states of america
where she contracted a rare autoimmune disease during which
she turned to poetry for comfort. she became an established poet
late in her life, publishing two volumes of poetry after 55 years of
working as a healer and medium, helping connect those who had
been estranged from their family members in the great refugee
crisis of 2016-2200. her work centered on ancestral memories,
the energy that lives within objects and the psychic space between
colony and place of origin. it is also worth noting that she never
used her government name and instead chose to use the last

five numbers of her refugee id card. she also refused to use the colonizers' hierarchy of capital and lowercase letters, insisting that all letters be equal once stating, "in my mothertongue the letters are connected, the way the letters stand in this language is a way of disconnection i am not interested in."

translator's note

by way of honoring her aesthetic, the translator has chosen to write about #05661's work using the same devices of language she applied.

© 2400

Invasius specius sapien reflects on the consequences of synthetic apertures

after Matthew Angelo Harrison

i was made invasive species beast of no nation a fish an ocean
pulsing between its jaws caught then thrown back my answers
garbled waxed a pitted bubblesong of zebra bones spread against
an empire of skinned accusation through plastic window and
conveyer belt i saw myself reflected brown pool mud eyes from
which god began creation n fur drippingt and basketmoufed in
every image they fevered to cache fingerprinted with furrowed
forehead grooves from the radiation of my many migrations
above the clouds and when i saw them infiltrating my first
and only homeland where i was born fala7a and trusting i with
retracted scales spreadedt paws speared through film and video
through their tinted windows i leaptt and clawed into their
tall airconditioned bus and laughed like hyena saliva driptt
at the sight of their oversoftt and overtlyt sunscreenedt flesh
ah ah they thought us savages but did not have eyes enough to
see themselves and as i tore a trail at them i moved so swiftly
through their theories of evolooshun: bird and beast, fish and
fauna, golden and gulping, feathered feral and scaled, nocturnal
and fecal but ah ah i was the one who became the consequence ah
the aperture to live in era where i knownt how they all loved to
watch themselves watch themselves so i leftt them stunnedt and
dangling by their ownt intestines to watch how i thrice evolved
quintuple helix amoeba bondt stoodt standing on mine own hind
legs and found myself staring at african specimen ah ah dearestt
skull of wildebeest collected and frozen was when i understood
i too might like to look at myself for in its orbits i saw it was the
city that made me now running through me the city where i made
my kill and didnt bury but instead made a spectacle of their flesh
i invasive species beast of no nation a being of no consequence

returning note no. 11

she overwhelms the senses you werent aware you had. and while youre distracted she slows or accelerates time depending on what she knows you need to see.

Gratitude

With thanks to the editors of the following publications in which these poems, sometimes in different versions, first appeared and or will be anthologized:

APOGEE, "of ritual"; *Behind the Lines: Poetry, War, & Peacemaking,* ")[[:".'.,:]]("; *Best American Experimental Writing (BAX) 2018,* "ghost purchase"; *Berkeley Poetry Review,* "afroarab cento"; *Bettering American Poetry 2016,* "poem to be read from right to left"; *Bettering American Poetry 2017,* "the middle east is missing"; *BOMB,* "freewrite for an audience"; "in the first world"; "poem that wrote me into beast in order to be read"; "photographs not taken"; *BreakBeat Poets: Black Girl Magic,* "poem that wrote me into beast in order to be read"; *The Felt,* "ha"; *The Lifted Brow,* "you got the keys, keys, keys" and ")[[:".'.,:]];("; *Foundry Journal,* "generation of feeling"; "write this instead"; *Hyperallergic,* "the middle east is missing"; *Tinderbox,* "ghost purchase"; *Winter Tangerine,* "poem to be read from right to left."

Gratitude to the One.

my mother, my mother, my mother, my mother, my father.

my brothers: hatem and yaser — you already know, this book is for you, my first accomplices and readers.

dear friends and mentors: tavonne s. carson; hayan charara; kyle dacuyan; eman elsheikh; roberto garcia; ysabel gonzalez; dr. jacobson; randa jarrar; bhanu kapil; rami karim; ricardo maldonado!; philip metres; jennifer obidike; xandria phillips; sahar romani; monica sok; calvin walds; and jenny xie.

my teachers, for all seen and unseen labor: elmaz abinader; cheryl boyce-taylor; jay deshpande; amber flora thomas; rigoberto gonzález; jason koo; tracie morris; miller oberman; willie perdomo; evie shockley; lyrae van clief-stefanon; simone white; and kevin young.

Nightboat Books for believing in this project and taking it on. Endless thanks to Stephen Motika, Kazim Ali, Lindsey Boldt, and Andrea Abi-Karam. Thank you HR Hegnauer for your patient attention in relaying this experience through design and to Seif Hamid for helping me achieve this cover vision.

and to the following communities and spaces for all you've gifted me: Asian American Writers' Workshop; Brooklyn Poets; Cave Canem Foundation; New York Foundation for the Arts: Immigrant Artist Program; Calabash: The Conversation Literary Fest; Poets House; The Poetry Project; RAWI; VONA/Voices; Wendy's Subway; and Winter Tangerine.

Notes

Writers and editors who incorrectly cite my book's title or misspell my name will be required to pay a fee of: 1. Donating to THE DREAM DEFENDERS or 2. Buying an additional 5-10 copies of this book. The size of the donation or the number of copies bought and hopefully, gifted (to schools, to libraries, etc.) should correlate with the total count of repeated errors. Receipt of this work confers your consent to this agreement.

"poem to be read from right to left" is written in a form invented by the poet called the Arabic.

The Arabic is a form that includes an Arabic letter with an Arabic footnote, and an Arabic numeral, preferably written right to left as the Arabic language is, and vehemently rejects you if you try to read it left to right. To vehemently reject, in this case, means to transfer the feeling of every time the poet has heard an English as Only Language speaker patronizingly utter in some variation the following phrase: "Oh, [so and so] is English as a Second Language…" As if it was a kind of weakness, nah.

"poem for brad who wants me to write about the pyramids" is dedicated to the people of Tahrir Square, the Arab Spring, and everyone protesting oppression the world over.

"poem for the beings who arrived" is a Zuihitsu dedicated to my Cave Canem fellowship Group C and borrows language from the works of Pablo Neruda, Fedor Alexandrovich, and Freak Nasty.

"freewrite for an audience" references my dear teacher Simone White and is dedicated to women everywhere but especially the women of our Cave Canem: Reading Hard Workshop.

"afroarab cento:" the poem is comprised entirely of lines borrowed from the following poets (in order of appearance): Etheridge Knight, Suheir Hammad, Ladan Osman, Philip Metres, Terrance Hayes, Farid Matuk, Evie Shockley, and June Jordan.

"if this was a different kind of story id tell you about the sea" is inspired by the short story, "The Sun, the Moon, the Stars" by Junot Díaz.

The first section of "ghost purchase" is written after my dear pressmate Hervé Guibert's *Ghost Image*.

References to Kanye West have been redacted in response to his recent statements, which are not worth repeating.

An earlier version of "Invasius specius sapien reflects on the consequences of synthetic apertures" was commissioned by the Studio Museum in Harlem and is based on Matthew Angelo Harrison's piece titled "consequences of synthetic apertures."

Thanks also to graffiti artist ESPO for the mural, "Love Letter to Brooklyn," from which the last section gets its title.

Suggested Further Reading

Targeted: Homeland Security and the Business of Immigration, Deepa Fernandes

Law and the Borders of Belonging in the Long Nineteenth Century United States, Barbara Young Welke

Tell Me How It Ends: An Essay in 40 Questions, Valeria Luiselli

About the Cover

Original cover art, "Calligrabirds," by Seif Hamid. A new vernacular of Arabic calligraphy hand drawn by the artist includes the author's first name in Arabic and calligraphic-specimens traveling upwards as calligrabirds, or when read as migrating downstream, calligrafish. The black lines represent permeable or "unsecured" borders and a few specimens are being targeted in red. Each calligraphic-specimen comprises an Arabic letter or word. The cover is dominated by a population of Calligraspecies that sing "laa" or speak dissent in the Arabic word for no, " ﻻ • (lā)." The title in English runs left to right as well as right to left, vertically.

so eat this black music and tell me how it taste now

The Game

ha

after Juvenile

that's you — a dark horse ha
that's you as a black unicorn
unrelenting and restless ha
you runnin before you had teeth ha
you delta spillin into mediterranean ha
how they raised us ha
i know i aint trippin auntie grillin fish ha
you ready to bust some embassy windows ha
you aint scared ha
you know how to play it ha

i know you aint just gonna let customs punk you ha
we was worlds ha
aint had a chance / but to make our own kind of free ha
straight up run you ha
you know who got that gibnah roomi ha
you know how to use a kanakah
shit aint hard as it seems ha
you keep your galabiyah clean ha
you got a lot of life ha
some of your cousins dope fiends ha
you made to leave ha
you dont care how bad it gets
you return ha
now you stuck here ha
you miss your cousins ha
this that survival haa

we drivin catchin air ha
thass the nile ha
yea you wish
abu simbel and karnak ha
everyone knows who our ancestors are ha
hatshepsut
hieroglyphs
now you learnin a new language like rosetta stone ha

you got the keys keys keys

an ode to DJ KHALED

you so naiive,
you sophisticated

you so spiritual
told larry king you pray 10 times a day, MORE THAN 10x a day
you pray in your head
all the time
now all the muslim boys
have a new line to impress the unkels with

must be why
you so fire
even water tried to claim you
remember when you got lost on a jetski in the dark?
that shit got what
like a billion some hits

snapchat should be payin you
instagram should be payin you
so you can put that money in a savings account
buy your mama a house
buy your whole family houses

you a hero
ridin in on a lion
watering your garden
talkin to flowers

we make memes of you:
            like, *when they want to ban palestinians*
            but then they would have to recognize palestine

i quote you in classrooms:
congratulations, you played yourself
and when the kids laugh
i tell them
you a genius / i appreciate you
you loyal
you
you on one
and anotha one

we the best

because of you i know i can put the hinges on the hands too

your voice smooth like olive oil from the holy land
beautiful, long lashed dark eyed heavy browed with
a beard made of our ancestors dreams
youre a version of the man i was raised to want
but could never stand to be with

still, i appreciate you
for what you undo

the bricks in amsterdam know your beats
heard you bumpin with drake in paris streets
weezy and you ridin through downtown cairo smog
and your outro fade like london fog
you so international
the kids in tel aviv throw back mai tais to "no new friends"

and nearby the palestinians dabke until they forget
they are palestinian
or rather, until they forget they are
occupied

yours is the rhythm they rebuild to
what do you say,
we give them all the keys?
major keys

back to their rightful homes.

photographs not taken

airbags opening during the crash,
a life saved;
DJ armed with two milk canisters,
when the three of us were still friends;
my mother's birthmark next to mine,
both on the same spot above our right knees,
hers brown on white,
mine white on brown,
proof: i am negative of her image;
flames moving upwards from the charcoal,
singeing my eyebrows and eyelashes;
flames that lit nashwa's soft sweater,
we were playing with sparklers in bideen;
flames in a trash bin, a homeless man,
winter in mansurah;
train light reflecting on rails when it is still arriving;
train light reflecting on walls when it is still arriving;
my mother when she was younger than me;
my father when he was younger than me;
my youngest brother's hand reaching out of the bathroom door,
open and waiting for a towel;
the Green Day CD my father threw out the window,
lying on the side of US131;
my grandmother tucked in for her afternoon nap,
the light in her window,
the light the day i left;
mezo's big toe,
before i left;
all the dawns i slept through,

before i left;
my own face,
looking back at his,
before i left;
your face,
the one
reading this.

MARWA HELAL is the author of the chapbook *I Am Made To Leave I Am Made To Return* and winner of *BOMB* Magazine's Biennial Contest. Born in Al Mansurah, Egypt, Helal currently lives in Brooklyn, New York.

Nightboat Books

Nightboat Books, a nonprofit organization, seeks to develop audiences for writers whose work resists convention and transcends boundaries. We publish books rich with poignancy, intelligence, and risk. Please visit our website, www.nightboat.org, to learn about our titles and how you can support our future publications.

The following individuals have supported the publication of this book. We thank them for their generosity and commitment to the mission of Nightboat Books:

Kazim Ali
Anonymous
Photios Giovanis
Elenor & Thomas Kovachevich
Elizabeth Motika
Leslie Scalapino – O Books Fund
Benjamin Taylor
Jerrie Whitfield & Richard Motika

In addition, this book has been made possible, in part, by grants from the National Endowment for the Arts and the New York State Council on the Arts Literature Program.

RECEIVED FEB – – 2020